God's Little Instruction Book For Dads

Wisdom, strength and humour
for the greatest job on earth

Marshall Pickering
An Imprint of HarperCollins*Publishers*

———————————— •◆• ————————————

God's Little Instruction Book for Dads is an inspirational
collection of memorable quotations and verses from the Bible
that will enable you to maximize the joys and minimize the
trials of fatherhood!

Each page brings you tried and tested human insight and
the timeless wisdom of the Bible in powerful combination,
designed to help you become the best father possible to
your children.

We hope that you enjoy and treasure this book
whether you are a father-to-be or an old hand!

The Publishers

———————————— •◆• ————————————

Marshall Pickering is an Imprint of
HarperCollinsReligious
Part of HarperCollins Publishers
77-85 Fulham Palace Road, London W6 8JB

First published in the USA in 1994 by Honor Books, Inc.
First published in Great Britain in 1995 by Marshall Pickering
1 3 5 7 8 9 10 8 6 4 2

A catalogue record for this book is available from the British Library.

Printed and bound in Great Britain by HarperCollinsManufacturing Glasgow

CONDITIONS OF SALE

There are many ways to measure success;
not the least of which is the way your child
describes you when talking to a friend.

UNKNOWN

A child's glory is his father

PROVERBS 17:6B TLB

A young successful attorney said:
The greatest gift I ever received was a gift I
got one Christmas when my Dad gave me
a small box. Inside was a note saying,
"Son, this year I will give you 365 hours,
an hour every day after dinner."
My Dad not only kept his promise, he said,
but every year he renewed it and it's the

greatest gift I ever had in my life.
I am the result of his time.

*Therefore be careful how you walk, not as unwise men,
but as wise, making the most of your time....*

EPHESIANS 5:15,16 NAS

How to curb juvenile delinquency:
1. Take time with your children.
2. Set your children a good example.

*....but be thou an example of the believers, in word,
in conversation,
in charity, in spirit, in faith, in purity.*

1 TIMOTHY 4:12

3. Give your children ideals for living.
4. Have a lot of activities planned.
5. Discipline your children.
6. Teach them about God.

BILLY GRAHAM

*Train up a child the way he should go:
and when he is old, he will not depart from it.*

PROVERBS 22:6

"Do you remember your father?" asked the judge sternly, "that father whom you have disgraced?" The prisoner answered: "I remember him perfectly. When I went to him for advice or companionship, he would look up from his book on the law of trusts, and say, 'Run away, boy, I am busy.' My father finished his book and here I am."

T. DeWitt Talmadge

And, ye fathers, provoke not your children to wrath: but bring them up in the nurture and admonition of the Lord.

EPHESIANS 6:4

The way each day will look to you all starts with *who* you're looking to.

UNKNOWN

I will lift up mine eyes unto the hills,
from whence cometh my help.
My help cometh from the Lord,
which made heaven and earth.

PSALM 121:1,2

The greatest thing a father can do for his children is to love their mother.

So ought men to love their wives as their own bodies. He that loveth his wife loveth himself.

If you want your child to accept your values when he reaches his teen years, then you must be worthy of his respect during his younger days.

JAMES DOBSON

....a model for you, that you might follow our example.

2 THESSALONIANS 3:9 NAS

A child is not likely to find a father in God unless he finds something of God in his father.

GLEN WHEELER

Be ye followers of me, even as I also am of Christ.

1 CORINTHIANS 11:1

A father's words are like a thermostat that
sets the temperature in the house.

PAUL LEWIS

Death and life are in the power of the tongue:
and they that love it shall eat the fruit thereof.

PROVERBS 18:21

While I don't minimize the vital role played by a mother, I believe a successful family begins with her husband.

JAMES DOBSON

He must be one who manages his own household well, keeping his children under control with all dignity.

1 TIMOTHY 3:4 NAS

Happy is the child who happens in upon
his parent from time to time to see him on
his knees, ...or going aside regularly,
to keep times with the Lord.

LARRY CHRISTENSON

....let the heart of them rejoice that seek the Lord.
Seek the Lord,
and his strength: seek his face evermore.

PSALM 105:3,4

When God measures a man, he puts the
tape around the heart instead of the head.

*....for the Lord seeth not as man seeth; for man looketh
on the outward appearance,
but the Lord looketh on the heart.*

1 SAMUEL 16:7

O, Lord....build me a son whose heart will be clear, whose goal will be high, a son who will master himself before he seeks to master other men; one who will reach into the future, yet never forget the past.

GENERAL DOUGLAS MACARTHUR

A wise son brings joy to his father....

PROVERBS 10:1 NIV

Too much love never spoils children.
Children become spoiled when we
substitute "presents" for "presence".

DR ANTHONY P. WITHAM

*We loved you dearly — so dearly that we gave you
not only God's message, but our own lives too.*

1 THESSALONIANS 2:8 TLB

Live truth instead of professing it.

ELBERT HUBBARD

But be ye doers of the word, and not hearers only, deceiving your own selves.

JAMES 1:22

Impossibilities vanish when a man
and his god confront a mountain.

ROBERT SCHULLER

....but with God all things are possible.

MATTHEW 19:26

For many little girls, life with father is a dress rehearsal for love and marriage.

DAVID JEREMIAH

Those things, which ye have both learned,
and received, and heard,
and seen in me, do: and the God of peace
shall be with you.

PHILIPPIANS 4:9

My primary role is not to be the boss
and just look good but to be a servant
leader who enables and enhances my
family to be their best.

TIM HANSEL

Let this mind be in you, which was also in Christ Jesus:
....(who) took upon him the form of a servant....

PHILIPPIANS 2:5,7

We too often love things and use people,
when we should be using things and
loving people.

UNKNOWN

Be devoted to one another in brotherly love.
Honour one another above yourselves.

ROMANS 12:10 NIV

The kind of man who thinks that helping with the dishes is beneath him will also think that helping with the baby is beneath him, and then he certainly is not going to be a very successful father.

ELEANOR ROOSEVELT

....but whoever wishes to become great among you shall be your servant.

MATTHEW 20:26 NAS

The best things you can give children,
next to good habits, are good memories.

SYDNEY J. HARRIS

The memory of the righteous is blessed....

PROVERBS 10:7 NAS

Honour is better than honours.

ABRAHAM LINCOLN

....for them that honour me I will honour....

SAMUEL 2:30

It may be hard on some fathers not to have a son, but it is much harder on a boy not to have a father.

SARA GILBERT

Withhold not good from them to whom it is due, when it is in the power of thine hand to do it.

PROVERBS 3:27

It is not what a man does that determines
whether his work is sacred or secular,
it is why he does it.

A. W. TOZER

*Whatever you do, work at it with all your heart,
as working for the Lord, not for men .... It is the Lord
Christ you are serving.*

COLOSSIANS 3:23,24 NIV

The most effective thing we can do for our children and families is pray for them.

ANTHONY EVANS

Devote yourselves to prayer, keeping alert in it with an attitude of thanksgiving.

COLOSSIANS 4:2 NAS

A father should never make distinctions between his children.

UNKNOWN.

For there is no respect of persons with God.

ROMANS 2:11

Character is what you are in the dark.

DWIGHT L. MOODY

The integrity of the upright shall guide them....

PROVERBS 11:3

One hundred years from now it won't matter if you got that big break....or finally traded up to a Mercedes. It will greatly matter, one hundred years from now, that you made a commitment to Jesus Christ.

DAVID SHIBLEY

For what is a man profited, if he shall gain the whole world, and lose his own soul?....

MATTHEW 16:26

You cannot teach a child to take care of himself unless you will let him try .... He will make mistakes; and out of these mistakes will come his wisdom.

HENRY WARD BEECHER

And all thy children shall be taught of the Lord; and great shall be the peace of thy children.

ISAIAH 54:13

He who sacrifices his conscience to ambition burns a picture to obtain the ashes.

UNKNOWN

Holding faith, and a good conscience; which some having put away concerning faith have made shipwreck.

1 TIMOTHY 1:19

The ultimate measure of a man is not where he stands in moments of comfort and convenience, but where he stands at times of challenge and controversy.

MARTIN LUTHER KING

If thou faint in the day of adversity, thy strength is small.

PROVERBS 24:10

If you tell the truth, you don't have to remember anything.

MARK TWAIN

*A truthful witness gives honest testimony,
but a false witness tells lies.*

PROVERBS 12:17 NIV

When we love something it is of value to us, and when something is of value to us we spend time with it, time enjoying it and time taking care of it.

M. SCOTT PECK

And I will very gladly spend and be spent for you....

2 CORINTHIANS 12:15

Nothing I've ever done has given me more joys and rewards than being a father to my children.

BILL COSBY

*Lo, children are an heritage of the Lord:
and the fruit of the womb is his reward.*

PSALM 127:3

Trust in yourself and you are doomed to disappointment;....trust in money and you may have it taken from you....but trust in God, and you are never to be confounded in time or eternity.

D.L. MOODY

It is better to take refuge in the Lord than to trust in man.

PSALM 118:8 NIV

The superior man....stands erect by bending above the fallen. He rises by lifting others.

ROBERT GREEN INGERSOLL

And we urge you, brethen, admonish the unruly, encourage the fainthearted, help the weak, be patient with all men.

1 THESSALONIANS 5:14 NAS

Children spell "Love"....T-i-m-e.

DR ANTHONY P WITHAM

Don't be fools; be wise; make the most of
every opportunity
you have for doing good.

EPHESIANS 5:16 TLB

It is better to bind your children to you
by a feeling of respect, and by gentleness,
than by fear.

TERENCE

....thy gentleness hath made me great.

PSALM 18:35

The best time for you to hold your tongue
is the time you feel you must say
something or bust.

JOSH BILLINGS

*Don't talk so much. You keep putting your foot
in your mouth. Be sensible and turn off the flow!*

PROVERBS 10:19 TLB

Laughter is the shortest distance
between two people.

VICTOR BORGE

*The light in the eyes (of him whose heart is joyful)
rejoices the hearts of others....*

PROVERBS 15:30 AMP

If you keep telling your son something's wrong with him, sooner or later he'll believe it. Follow every "That's wrong" by saying what's right.

JOHN E. ANDERSON

And I myself also am persuaded of you, my brethren, that ye also are full of goodness, filled with all knowledge....

ROMANS 15:14

You can't do much about your ancestors
but you can influence your descendants
enormously.

ANONYMOUS

....but as for me and my house, we will serve the Lord.

JOSHUA 24:15

Every dad is the family role model,
whether he wants the job or not.

DENNIS RAINEY

*....in order to offer ourselves as a model for you,
that you might follow our example.*

2 THESSALONIANS 3:9 NAS

Children are like clocks; they must be allowed to run.

DR JAMES DOBSON

Fathers....do not be hard on them (children)
or harass them;
lest they become discouraged ....

COLOSSIANS 3:21 AMP

The child that never learns to obey his parents in the home will not obey God or man out of the home.

SUSANNE WESLEY

Children, obey your parents in the Lord: for this is right.

EPHESIANS 6:1

By profession I am a soldier and take pride in that fact, but I am prouder to be a father.

GENERAL DOUGLAS MACARTHUR

I have great confidence in you: I take great pride in you....
2 CORINTHIANS 7:4 NIV

The strongest evidence of love is sacrifice.

CAROLINE FRY

*For God so loved the world, that he gave his
only begotten Son, that
whosoever believeth in him should not perish,
but have everlasting life.*

JOHN 3:16

Govern a family as you would cook
a small fish — very gently.

And the servant of the Lord must not strive;
but be gentle unto all men....

2 TIMOTHY 2:24

Words have an awesome impact.
The impressions made by a father's voice
can set in motion an entire trend of life.

GORDON MACDONALD

Death and life are in the power of the tongue;
and they that love it shall eat the fruit thereof.

PROVERBS 18:21

Like father, like son:
every good tree maketh good fruits.

WILLIAM LANGLAND

Even so every good tree bringeth forth good fruit....

MATTHEW 7:17

An infallible way to make your child
miserable is to satisfy all his demands.

HENRY HOME (LORD KAMES)

The rod and reproof give wisdom:
but a child left to himself bringeth....shame.

PROVERBS 29:15

Performance under stress is one test of effective leadership. It may also be the proof of accomplishment when it comes to evaluating the quality of a father.

GORDON MACDONALD

Cast thy burden upon the Lord, and he shall sustain thee: he shall never suffer the righteous to be moved.

PSALM 55:22

The man who fears no truths has nothing to fear from lies.

THOMAS JEFFERSON

....may your love and your truth always protect me.

PSALM 40:11 NIV

Men will spend their health getting wealth;
then gladly pay all they have earned
to get health back.

MIKE MURDOCK

*People who want to get rich fall into temptation
and a trap and into many foolish and harmful desires
that plunge men into ruin and destruction.*

1 TIMOTHY 6:9 NIV

Many a man spanks his children for things his own father should have spanked him for.

DON MARQUIS

Withhold not correction from the child:
for if thou beatest him
with the rod, he shall not die.
Thou shalt beat him with the rod,
and shalt deliver his soul from hell.

PROVERBS 23:13,14

The first duty of love is to listen.

PAUL TILLICH

Wherefore, my beloved brethren,
let every man be swift to hear....

JAMES 1:19

He that will have his son have respect for him and his orders, must himself have a great reverence for his son.

JOHN LOCKE

Be devoted to one another in brotherly love; give preference to one another in honour.

ROMANS 12:10 NAS

No person was ever honoured for what
he received. Honour has been the reward
for what he gave.

CALVIN COOLIDGE

....the righteous giveth and spareth not.

PROVERBS 21:26

Responsibility is the thing people dread most of all. Yet it is the one thing in the world that develops us, gives us manhood....fibre.

FRANK CRANE

Blessed is that servant, whom his lord when he cometh shall find so doing.

LUKE 12:43

....We can either grace our children, or damn them with unrequited wounds which never seem to heal....Men, as fathers you have such power!

R. KENT HUGHES

Death and life are in the power of the tongue: and they that love it shall eat the fruit thereof.

PROVERBS 18:21

Perhaps once in a hundred years a person
may be ruined by excessive praise,
but surely once every minute someone
dies inside for lack of it.

CECIL G. OSBORNE

Let no corrupt communication proceed out of your mouth,
but that which is good to the use of edifying,
that it may minister grace unto the hearers.

EPHESIANS 4:29

To become a father is not hard,
to be a father is, however.

WILHELM BUSCH

*Get all the advice you can and be wise
the rest of your life.*

PROVERBS 19:20 TLB

Opportunities for meaningful
communication between fathers
and sons must be created.
And it's work to achieve.

JAMES DOBSON

To every thing there is a season,
....a time to keep silence, and a time to speak.

ECCLESIASTES 3:1,7

Big people monopolize the listening.
Small people monopolize the talking.

DAVID SCHWARTZ

Seest thou a man that is hasty in his words?
there is more hope of a fool than of him.

PROVERBS 29:20

Don't be a lion in your own house.

UNKNOWN

Not lording it over those entrusted to you....

1 PETER 5:3 NIV

Train your child in the way in which you know you should have gone yourself.

C. H. SPURGEON

I will instruct thee and teach thee in the way which thou shalt go: I will guide thee with mine eye.

PSALM 32:8

Attention men: before you criticize another,
look closely at your sister's brother!

UNKNOWN

Do not judge lest you be judged.
For in the way you judge, you will be
judged; and by your standard of measure,
it will be measured to you.

MATTHEW 7:1,2 NAS

God sends no one away except those
who are full of themselves.

D.L. MOODY

....for God resisteth the proud,
and giveth grace to the humble.

1 PETER 5:5

There is no more vital calling or vocation for men than fathering.

JOHN R. THROOP

I press toward the mark for the prize of the high calling of God in Christ Jesus.

PHILIPPIANS 3:14

The measure of a man is not what he does on Sunday, but rather who he is Monday to Saturday.

UNKNOWN

....that you may live worthy of the Lord
and may please him
in every way: bearing fruit in every good work....

COLOSSIANS 1:10 NIV

The world is blessed most by men who do things, and not by those who merely talk about them.

JAMES OLIVER

But be ye doers of the word, and not hearers only, deceiving your own selves.

JAMES 1:22

Authority without wisdom is like a heavy axe without an edge, fitter to bruise than polish.

ANNE BRADSTREET

....the authority the Lord gave me for building you up, not for tearing you down.

1 CORINTHIANS 13:10 NIV

Dad, when you come home at night with only shattered pieces of your dreams, your little one can mend them like new with two magic words — "Hi, Dad!"

ALAN BECK

For we have great joy and consolation in thy love....

PHILEMON 7

Unconditional love is loving a child no matter what....we expect him to be, and most difficult, no matter how he acts.

ROSS CAMPBELL

But show me unfailing kindness like that of the Lord as long as I live....

1 SAMUEL 20:14 NIV

The value of marriage is not that adults produce children but that children produce adults.

PETER DeVRIES

When I was a child, I spake as a child,
I understood as a child, I thought
as a child: but when I became a man,
I put away childish things.

1 CORINTHIANS 13:11

The best way to teach character is
to have it around the house.

*A righteous man who walks in his integrity —
how blessed are his sons after him.*

PROVERBS 20:7 NAS

The man who wins may have been
counted out several times, but he
didn't hear the referee.

H.E. JANSEN

For though a righteous man falls seven times,
he rises again....

PROVERBS 24:16 NIV

Keep company with good men and good
men you will imitate.

UNKNOWN

*Iron sharpeneth iron; so a man sharpeneth
the countenance of his friend.*

PROVERBS 27:17

The great man is he who does not lose
his child's heart.

MENCIUS

And he shall turn the heart of the fathers to the children,
and the heart of the children to their fathers....

MALACHI 4:6

An ounce of loving role modelling is worth
a pound of parental pressure.

V. GILBERT BEERS

In everything set them an example by doing what is good.
TITUS 2:7 NIV

Every child comes with the message that
God is not yet discouraged of man.

TAGORE

*What is man, that thou are mindful of him?
and the son of man,
that thou visitest him? for thou hast made him a little lower
than the angels, and hast crowned him with glory
and honour.*

PSALM 8:4,5

My father is the standard by which all subsequent men in my life have been judged.

KATHRYN MCCARTHY GRAHAM

....*leaving us an example, that ye should follow his steps.*

1 PETER 2:21

Some parents bring up their children on
thunder and lightning, but thunder and
lightning never yet made anything grow.

UNKNOWN

....you should practise tenderhearted mercy
and kindness to others....
Most of all, let love guide your life....

COLOSSIANS 3:12,14 TLB

My Dad and I hunted and fished together.
How could I get angry with this man
who took the time to be with me?

JAMES DOBSON

Honour thy father....

EXODUS 20:12

Unless a father accepts his faults he will most certainly doubt his virtues.

HUGH PRATHER

....he hath made us accepted in the beloved.

EPHESIANS 1:6

What was silent in the father speaks in the son, and often I have found the son the unveiled secret of the father.

And he did that which was right in the sight of the Lord....as Joash his father did.

2 KINGS 14:3

Gentlemen, try not to become men of success. Rather, become men of value.

Albert Einstein

The just man walketh in his integrity....

Proverbs 20:7

A man's children and his garden both reflect the amount of weeding done during the growing season.

UNKNOWN

He who spares his rod hates his son,
but he who loves him disciplines him diligently.

PROVERBS 13:24 NAS

If it is desirable that children be kind, appreciative and pleasant, then those qualities should be taught - not hoped for.

JAMES DOBSON

For the commandment is a lamp; and the law is light; and reproofs of instruction are the way of life.

PROVERBS 6:23

Our children give us the opportunity to become the parents we always wish we had.

NANCY SAMALIN

Therefore all things whatsoever ye would that men should do to you, do ye even so to them....

MATTHEW 7:12

To be successful in the family the father
must have the welfare of each family
member at heart, and his decisions and plans
must be based upon what is best for them.

HELEN ANDELIN

Do nothing from selfishness or empty conceit,
but with humility of mind
let each of you regard one another as
more important than himself.

PHILIPPIANS 2:3 NAS

Children miss nothing in sizing up their parents. If you are only half-convinced of your beliefs, they will quickly discern that fact.

JAMES DOBSON

Let us hold fast the profession of our faith without wavering....

HEBREWS 10:23

Children are our most valuable
natural resource.

HERBERT HOOVER

Children are an heritage of the Lord....

PSALM 127:3

A young branch takes on all the bends
that one gives to it.

Train up a child in the way that he should go:
and when he is old, he will not depart from it.

PROVERBS 26:6

If there be any truer measure of a man than by what he does, it must be by what he gives.

ROBERT SOUTH

....It is more blessed to give than to receive.

ACTS 20:35

Men for the sake of getting a living
forget to live.

MARGARET FULLER

*It is vain for you to rise up early, to take rest late,
to eat the bread of
(anxious) toil - for He gives (blessings)
to His beloved in sleep.*

PSALM 127:2 AMP

If a man cannot be a Christian in the place where he is, he cannot be a Christian anywhere.

HENRY WARD BEECHER

Let your light so shine before men, that they may see your good works, and glorify your Father which is in heaven.

MATTHEW 5:16

You cannot live a perfect day without doing something for someone who will never be able to repay you.

JOHN WOODEN

And do not forget to do good and to share with others, for with such sacrifices God is pleased.

HEBREWS 13:16 NIV

From good parents comes a good son.

ARISTOTLE

A good tree cannot bear bad fruit....

MATTHEW 7:18 NIV

Among all the abuses of the world....
there is none worse than a negligent father.

STAFANO GUAZZO

*But you have neglected the more important
matters of the law — justice, mercy and faithfulness.*

MATTHEW 23:23C NIV

Children need love, especially when they do not deserve it.

HAROLD S. HULBERT

Therefore be imitators of God, as beloved children;
and walk in love,
just as Christ also loved you, and gave Himself up for us,
an offering and a sacrifice to God as a fragrant aroma.

EPHESIANS 5:1,2 NAS

Praise your children openly,
reprove them secretly.

W. CECIL

Correct thy son, and he shall give thee rest;
yea, he shall give delight unto thy soul.

PROVERBS 29:17

Every man is enthusiastic at times.
One man has enthusiasm for thirty minutes,
another has it for thirty days — but
it is the man that has it for thirty years
who makes a success of life.

Unknown

....let us run with perseverance the race marked out for us.

Hebrews 12:1 NIV

Measure wealth not by the things you have, but by the things you have for which you would not take money.

ANONYMOUS

....for a man's life consisteth not in the abundance of the things which he possesseth.

LUKE 12:15

It takes time to be a good father. It takes effort —trying, failing and trying again.

TIM HANSEL

And let us not get tired of doing what is right,
for after a while we will
reap a harvest of blessing if we don't get
discouraged and give up.

GALATIANS 6:9 TLB

Children desperately need to know —
and to hear in ways they understand and
remember — that they're loved and
valued by Mum and Dad.

GARY SMALLEY AND PAUL TRENT

....let us stop just saying we love people;
let us really love them,
and show it by our actions.

1 JOHN 3:18 TLB

Happiness is inward, and not outward; and so, it does not depend on what we have, but on what we are.

HENRY VAN DYKE

Beware! Don't always be wishing for what you don't have. For real life and real living are not related to how rich we are.

LUKE 12:15 TLB

The foolish man seeks happiness in the distance; the wise grows it under his feet.

JAMES OPENHEIM

....for I have learned, in whatsoever state I am, therewith to be content.

PHILIPPIANS 4:11

Self-esteem isn't a lesson you teach; it's a quality you nurture.

Dr Ronald Levant and John Kelly

....but bring them up in the nurture and admonition of the Lord.

Ephesians 6:4

When we do what we can,
God will do what we can't.

UNKNOWN

For with God nothing shall be impossible.

LUKE 1:37

Seek God first and the things
you want will seek you.

UNKNOWN

But seek ye first the kingdom of God,
and his righteousness;
and all these things shall be added unto you.

MATTHEW 6:33

The strength of a man consists in finding out the way God is going, and going that way.

HENRY WARD BEECHER

....I am the light of the world: he that followeth me shall not walk in darkness, but shall have the light of life.

JOHN 8:12

I owe almost everything to my father.

MARGARET THATCHER

Honour thy father....as the Lord thy God hath commanded thee....

DEUTERONOMY 5:16

The more a child becomes aware of a father's willingness to listen, the more a father will begin to hear.

GORDON MACDONALD

He that hath ears to hear, let him hear.

MATTHEW 11:15

Until you make peace with who you are,
you'll never be content with what you have.

DORIS MORTMAN

But godliness with contentment is great gain.

1 TIMOTHY 6:6

A gentleman is a *gentle man.*

UNKNOWN

And the servant of the Lord must not strive;
but be gentle unto all men....

2 TIMOTHY 2:24

(The called man) sees himself as a steward....he's obedient rather than ambitious, committed rather than competitive. For him, nothing is more important than pleasing the one who called him.

RICHARD EXLEY

....because we obey his commands and do what pleases him.

1 JOHN 3:22 NIV

If I take care of my character, my reputation will take care of itself.

DWIGHT L. MOODY

Righteousness guards the man of integrity....

PROVERBS 13:6 NIV

Remember, when your child has a tantrum,
don't have one of your own.

DR J. KURIANSKY

Cease from anger, and forsake wrath;
fret not thyself in any wise to do evil.

PSALM 37:8

Children are not so different from
kites....Children were created to fly.
But they need wind — the undergirding
and strength that comes from unconditional
love, encouragement and prayer.

GIGI GRAHAM TCHIVIDJIAN

....as a father deals with his own children, encouraging,
comforting and urging you to live lives worthy of God....

1 THESSALONIANS 2:11,12 NIV

....When these parenting years have passed, something precious will have flickered and gone out of my life. Thus, I am resolved to enjoy every day that remains in this fathering era.

JAMES DOBSON

Redeeming the time....

EPHESIANS 5:16

10 COMMANDMENTS FOR EFFECTIVE FATHERS

Fathers, do not exasperate your children, instead, bring them up in the training and instruction of the Lord.

EPHESIANS 6:4 NIV

1. Spend time with your children

Making the very most of the time —
buying up each opportunity....

EPHESIANS 5:16 AMP

2. Let your children know often that you love them just the way they are.

Wherefore, accept one another,
just as Christ also accepted us....

ROMANS 15:7 NAS

3. Discipline your children when they need it.

He who spares his rod hates his son,
but he who loves him disciplines him diligently.

PROVERBS 13:24 NAS

4. Pray with and for your children, regularly.

Wherefore also we pray always for you....

2 THESSALONIANS 1:11

5. Always be honest with your children.

A good man is known by his truthfulness;
a false man by deceit and lies.

PROVERBS 12:17 TLB

6. Love your children's mother.

*And you husbands, show the same kind of love
to your wives
as Christ showed to the Church when he died for her.*

EPHESIANS 5:25 TLB

7. Take time to listen to your children.

Let the wise listen and add to their learning....

PROVERBS 1:5 NIV

8. Encourage your children often.

Therefore encourage one another and build each other up....

1 THESSALONIANS 5:11 NIV

9. Celebrate your children's achievements.

Rejoice with them that do rejoice....

ROMANS 12:15

10. Be flexible with your children.

Be patient with each other, making allowance
for each other's faults because of your love.

EPHESIANS 4:2B

HUMOROUS QUOTES SECTION

A merry heart doeth good like a medicine....

PROVERBS 17:22

There is a right time for everything: A time to laugh....

ECCLESIASTES 3:1,4 TLB

There are three ways to get something done: do it yourself, hire someone, or forbid your kids to do it.

MONTA CRANE

A merry heart doeth good like a medicine....

PROVERBS 17:22

A father is someone who carries pictures
where his money used to be.

LION

There is a right time for everything: A time to laugh....
ECCLESIASTES 3:1,4 TLB

To men over 40: don't worry about losing hair; think of it as gaining face.

UNKNOWN

A merry heart doeth good like a medicine....

PROVERBS 17:22

Many a father wishes he were strong enough to tear a telephone book in two — especially if he has a teenage daughter.

GUY LOMBARDO

There is a right time for everything: A time to laugh....

ECCLESIASTES 3:1,4 TLB

A father is a person who is forced to endure childbirth without an anaesthetic.

ROBERT C. SAVAGE

A merry heart doeth good like a medicine....

PROVERBS 17:22

Before I got married, I had six theories about bringing up children; now I have six children and no theories.

LORD ROCHESTER

There is a right time for everything: A time to laugh....
ECCLESIASTES 3:1,4 TLB

Fatherhood is pretending the present you
love most is soap-on-a-rope.

BILL COSBY

A merry heart doeth good like a medicine....

PROVERBS 17:22

Old boys have their playthings as well
as young ones; the difference is only in
the price.

BENJAMIN FRANKLIN

There is a right time for everything: A time to laugh....

ECCLESIASTES 3:1,4 TLB

A major problem these days is how to save
money for your children's college education
when you're still paying for yours.

UNKNOWN

A merry heart doeth good like a medicine....

PROVERBS 17:22

A boy becomes an adult three years before his parents think he does, and about two years after he thinks he does.

LEWIS B. HERSHEY

There is a right time for everything: A time to laugh....

ECCLESIASTES 3:1,4 TLB

Before marriage, a man will lie awake
all night thinking about something you
said; after marriage, he'll fall asleep before
you finish saying it.

HELEN ROWLAND

A merry heart doeth good like a medicine....

PROVERBS 17:22

Is it not strange that he who has no children brings them up so well?

UNKNOWN

There is a right time for everything: A time to laugh....

ECCLESIASTES 3:1,4 TLB

The young man knows the rules, but the old man knows the exceptions.

OLIVER WENDELL HOLMES

A merry heart doeth good like a medicine....

PROVERBS 17:22

Father: a man who can't get on the phone, into the bathroom, or out of the house.

ANONYMOUS

There is a right time for everything: A time to laugh....

ECCLESIASTES 3:1,4 TLB

In a perfect world....teenagers would much rather work on the lawn than talk on the telephone.

JOHN GRATTON

A merry heart doeth good like a medicine....

PROVERBS 17:22

When I was a boy of fourteen my father
was so ignorant I could hardly stand to have
the old man around. But when I got to be
twenty-one I was astonished at how much
the old man had learned in seven years.

MARK TWAIN

There is a right time for everything: A time to laugh....

ECCLESIASTES 3:1,4 TLB

A father is a thing that growls when it feels good....and laughs very loud when it's scared half to death.

PAUL HARVEY

A merry heart doeth good like a medicine....

PROVERBS 17:22

It now costs more to amuse a child than
it once did to educate his father.

H.V. PROCHNOW

There is a right time for everything: A time to laugh....

ECCLESIASTES 3:1,4 TLB

In a perfect world....children on trips would say, "Isn't riding in the car fun!" and then they'd fall asleep.

JOHN GRATTON

A merry heart doeth good like a medicine....

PROVERBS 17:22

Fathers are what give daughters away to other men who aren't nearly good enough....so they can have grandchildren that are smarter than anybody's.

PAUL HARVEY

There is a right time for everything: A time to laugh....
ECCLESIASTES 3:1,4 TLB